MONUMENTAL MILESTONES
GREAT EVENTS OF MODERN TIMES

The Story of the Attack on Pearl Harbor

Two U.S. destroyers reflect the damage inflicted by Japan.

Mitchell Lane
PUBLISHERS

P.O. Box 196
Hockessin, Delaware 19707

Titles in the Series

The Dawn of Aviation:
The Story of the Wright Brothers

The Story of the Attack on Pearl Harbor

Breaking the Sound Barrier:
The Story of Chuck Yeager

Top Secret: The Story of the
Manhattan Project

The Story of the Holocaust

The Civil Rights Movement

Exploring the North Pole:
The Story of Robert Edwin
Peary and Matthew Henson

The Story of the Great Depression

The Cuban Missile Crisis:
The Cold War Goes Hot

The Fall of the Berlin Wall

Disaster in the Indian Ocean
Tsunami 2004

The Story of the Attack on Pearl Harbor

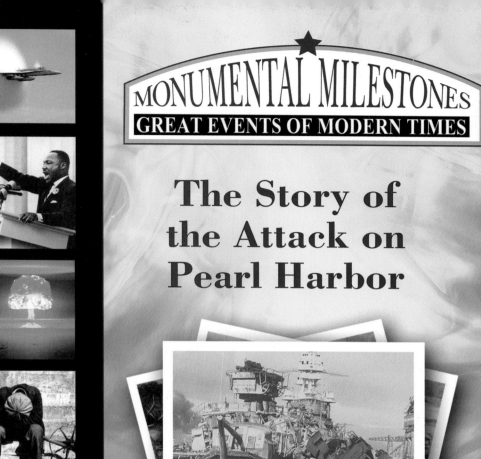

The USS *Downes* (left) and the USS *Cassin* were attacked by Japan.

Jim Whiting

Mitchell Lane
PUBLISHERS

Printing   2   3   4   5   6   7   8

Library of Congress Cataloging-in-Publication Data

Whiting, Jim, 1943–

The story of the attack on Pearl Harbor / by Jim Whiting.

p. cm. — (Monumental milestones)

Includes bibliographical references and index.

ISBN 1-58415-397-0 (library bound)

1. World War, 1939–1945—Pacific Area—Juvenile literature. 2. Pearl Harbor (Hawaii), Attack on, 1941—Juvenile literature. 3. World War, 1939–1945—United States—Juvenile literature. 4. World War, 1939–1945—Japan—Juvenile literature. I. Title. II. Series.

D767.W473 2005

940.54'26—dc22

2004030309

ISBN 13: 9781584153979

ABOUT THE AUTHOR: Jim Whiting has been a remarkably versatile and accomplished journalist, writer, editor and photographer for more than 30 years. A voracious reader since early childhood, Mr. Whiting has written and edited about 200 non-fiction children's books. His subjects range from authors to zoologists and include contemporary pop icons and classical musicians, saints and scientists, emperors and explorers. Representative titles include *The Life and Times of Franz Liszt*, *The Life and Times of Julius Caesar*, *Charles Schulz*, *The Cuban Missile Crisis: The Cold War Goes Hot*, and *Juan Ponce de Leon*.

Other career highlights are a lengthy stint publishing *Northwest Runner*, the first piece of original fiction to appear in *Runners World* magazine, hundreds of descriptions and venue photographs for *America Online*, e-commerce product writing, sports editor for the *Bainbridge Island Review*, light verse in a number of magazines, and acting as the official photographer for the *Antarctica Marathon*.

He lives in Washington state with his wife and two teenage sons.

PHOTO CREDITS: Cover, pp. 1, 3, 6, 20, 22, 26, 28, 32, 37—Naval Historical Center; pp. 10, 34—Sharon Beck; p. 12—Library of Congress.

PUBLISHER'S NOTE: This story is based on the author's extensive research, which he believes to be accurate. Documentation of such research is contained on page 47. PLB4

Contents

The Story of the Attack on Pearl Harbor
Jim Whiting

*For Your Information

This aerial photo shows how Pearl Harbor appeared on October 30, 1941.

No one there at the time could have imagined the horror that would strike the base less than six weeks later. This view looks to the southwest. It clearly shows the narrow channel that leads to the open sea in the top center of the photo. The Ford Island Naval Air Station is just beneath the channel.

A Morning of Missed Warnings

Ensign R. C. McCloy carefully scanned the dark waters just outside of Pearl Harbor with his binoculars. Pearl Harbor was the most important U.S. military installation on the Hawaiian island of Oahu (oh-WAH-hoo). It was about 0340 (3:40 A.M.) on December 7, 1941. McCloy was standing on the bridge of his ship, the minesweeper USS *Condor*. The vessel was on a routine patrol.

McCloy, like nearly every serviceman stationed at Pearl Harbor and several other military bases on Oahu, knew there was a good chance that his country would soon be at war with Japan. Like nearly every other serviceman, he couldn't imagine that the beginning of the war would involve him personally. Japan was thousands of miles away from Hawaii.

Military commanders were more concerned about the loyalty of the people of Japanese descent who lived in Hawaii than they were about Japanese nationals. When war broke out, they were afraid that some of them might try to commit acts of sabotage. To reduce that possibility, hundreds of aircraft on Oahu's airfields were out in the open and packed closely together. That made them easier to guard.

McCloy—and nearly every other serviceman—was wrong. About 300 miles north of him, hundreds of mechanics were swarming over more than 350 warplanes on six Japanese aircraft carriers. The carriers and their escorting warships had steamed undetected for more than a week since leaving Japan. In just over two hours, the planes would start taking off. Their destination was Oahu.

McCloy stiffened. Not far away he saw the unmistakable shape of a periscope. McCloy knew it wasn't an American submarine. They weren't allowed to be submerged in that area. Quickly he sent a message to the USS *Ward*, a destroyer patrolling nearby. The *Ward* was equipped for locating subs. Though it spent an hour searching, the *Ward* could not detect anything. Neither vessel sent a message ashore about what they were doing.

At about 0630, the supply ship USS *Antares* was preparing to enter the channel leading into Pearl Harbor. Lookouts aboard *Ward* and a Catalina patrol plane sighted a curious object just behind *Antares* and moving at the same speed. Soon they realized that it was a tiny, partially surfaced submarine. It was obviously trying to sneak into Pearl Harbor. The plane dropped smoke pots to mark the location. At 0645, *Ward*'s gunners opened fire. A shell hit the submarine and it began to sink. For good measure, *Ward* dropped several depth charges.

At 0654, *Ward* sent a short message in code to the shore station: "We have attacked, fired on, depth-bombed, and sunk submarine operating in defensive sea area."[1] The man who received the message took more than fifteen minutes to decode it, then passed it along to the officer on duty. The officer was alarmed. When he notified his superiors, they weren't. There had been a number of false alarms near Pearl Harbor in the past few weeks. Many phone calls went back and forth. In the confusion, some vital information was lost. One was that *Ward* had actually seen an enemy submarine. Another was that the ship had shot at the target.

Besides, the officers all knew that heavy concentrations of Japanese warships and troop transports had been observed off the coast of Siam (modern-day Thailand) and other locations in southern Asia thousands of miles away. It seemed obvious that the war would start there. None of the officers seemed especially concerned about *Ward*'s message. There would be plenty of time to verify the report.

At about the same time that *Ward* opened fire, a radar station on the northern coast of Oahu had picked up a single contact coming in from the north. The two army privates who were operating the station reported the contact. No one paid any attention. The contact seemed too small to matter.

About fifteen minutes later, the privates noticed a huge contact suddenly appear on their screen. They notified the officer in charge. Radar was still very new. The set had been installed only a few weeks earlier. Its reliability was still in question. The officer also knew that a flight of about a dozen B-17 bombers was due to arrive from the West Coast that morning. Even though the direction of the contact was different from the one the bombers would be using, the officer assumed that what the two men were reporting was the B-17s. He told them not to worry about it.

The two privates decided to continue tracking the incoming aircraft to get practice. When the contact disappeared into the electronic shadow cast by the hills of the island, the men shut down their radar. It was time to go off duty and have breakfast.

Earlier that morning, U.S. General George C. Marshall had sent a telegram from his office in Washington, D.C. It was addressed to General Walter Short, the commander of the army forces on Oahu. Marshall wanted Short to know that Japanese diplomats in Washington, D.C., were delivering a message at 1300 (1:00 P.M.) that afternoon. That would be 0730 in Honolulu. Because the diplomats had been so precise about the time, Marshall believed that a Japanese attack against the United States was likely to occur at about that time. He thought the Philippine Islands would be the target, but wanted all U.S. forces in the Pacific to be aware of the timing and be especially vigilant.

When Marshall's message arrived in Honolulu, it was placed inside an envelope that gave no indication of its importance. There was no reason for the messenger who came into the telegraph office at 0730 to give it special treatment. He tucked it into his bag with dozens of other telegrams. He got onto his motorcycle and began his deliveries. There would be plenty of time to deliver Marshall's message.

By then, thousands of sailors on the dozens of ships in the harbor were brushing the sleep out of their eyes. They began assembling on deck for the ceremonial raising of the colors. Many were looking forward to going ashore. After a hard week of training at sea, it was time to relax.

None of them suspected that there would be no relaxation on that sunny Sunday morning. At 0753, a Japanese airman high above Pearl Harbor exultantly radioed, "Tora! Tora! Tora!" In Japanese, the words meant "Tiger! Tiger! Tiger!"

The words also meant that time had run out for the Americans.

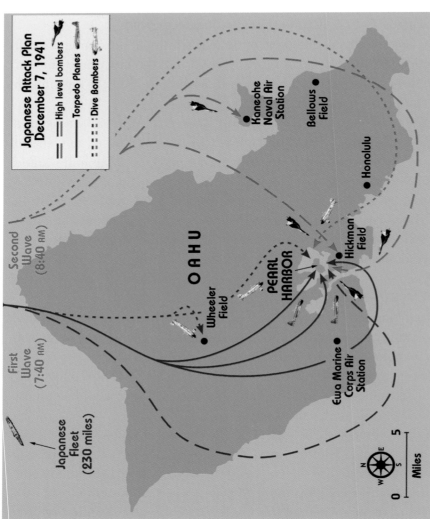

**Japanese Attack Plan
December 7, 1941**

= = = High level bombers
——— Torpedo Planes
· · · · · : Dive Bombers

First
Wave
(7:40 AM)

Second
Wave
(8:40 AM)

Japanese
Fleet
(230 miles)

OAHU

Wheeler
Field

PEARL
HARBOR

Ewa Marine
Corps Air
Station

Hickman
Field

Honolulu

Bellows
Field

Kaneohe
Naval Air
Station

0   5
Miles

This map of the island of Oahu, part of the Hawaiian islands, shows the routes taken by the two waves of Japanese planes on the morning of December 7, 1941. Torpedo planes were only in the first wave. Because they had to fly very low to make their attacks, they would have made easy targets for hundreds of angry American gunners in the second wave.

**Secretary of State
James Blaine**

American whaling ships and missionaries began visiting the Hawaiian Islands early in the nineteenth century. They were followed by U.S. sugar planters, who soon exerted a large influence economically and politically. In 1881, Secretary of State James Blaine said, "The United States regards the Hawaii group as essentially a part of the American system of states. . . . We could not regard the intrusion of any non-American interest in Hawaii as consistent with our relations."[2]

By then, about 20,000 Japanese had already settled on Hawaii. They far outnumbered white residents. Led by Sanford Dole and backed by a force of U.S. Marines, a group of Americans seized control in an 1893 coup, even though most Hawaiians opposed the move. The new government limited the right to vote to their fellow whites and native Hawaiians, denying it to the Japanese.

Not surprisingly, the Japanese protested. They were also very interested in Hawaii as a base for future expansion. "Where else but in Hawaii can the Japanese race hope to compete truly and frontally with the white race?" asked Japanese author Setsu Nagasawa.[3] Their concerns became greater when several passenger ships carrying hundreds of Japanese wanting to settle in the islands were turned away in 1897. The Japanese government immediately sent a warship to Hawaii.

This reaction gave a boost to American politicians, who had been advocating formal annexation for several decades. Annexation received a further boost in 1898. American ships and troops stopped at Pearl Harbor—which had long been regarded as an excellent harbor—in 1898 on their way to the Philippine Islands as part of the U.S. strategy in the Spanish-American War. The visit demonstrated the value of the islands. Congress passed a resolution approving annexation soon afterward. The Japanese were angry but decided that the issue didn't warrant starting a war. Ironically, annexation set off a new wave of Japanese emigration to Hawaii. The Japanese population exceeded 60,000 by the early 1900s.

Hawaii became a U.S. territory in 1900. Dole was the territory's first governor. Hawaii joined the Union as the fiftieth state in 1959.

Commodore Matthew Perry led the U.S. warships that forced Japan to open itself to trade with other nations.

Perry was the son of a naval officer. He had a long and distinguished career in the U.S. Navy. His brother, Oliver Hazard Perry, was equally distinguished. He led a squadron of U.S. ships in the Battle of Lake Erie during the War of 1812. His forces captured every British ship.

CHAPTER 2

The Long Road to War

The roots of the Pearl Harbor attack had been put down nearly ninety years earlier. With its victory in the Mexican-American War in 1848, the United States gained a huge chunk of territory, which included California. Bursting with optimism, the country wanted to expand its power and its possibilities for trade into the Pacific Ocean.

One obvious place was Japan. For nearly 250 years, the island nation had deliberately cut itself off from outside influence to preserve its social structure. Foreign ships were turned away. The ruling class were samurai warriors who were armed with swords. There were few guns of any type in Japan.

The country's isolation ended in July 1853, when Commodore Matthew Perry led a fleet of four American ships armed with powerful cannons into Tokyo Bay. The Japanese were powerless to resist. After a tense exchange, Perry sailed away. He said he would be back early the following year. He expected to make a deal.

He was as good as his word, reappearing the following year with an even larger fleet. Both sides looked down on the other. The Japanese considered Perry and his men to be unclean barbarians. The Americans thought the Japanese were backward.

There was no doubt about the winner. The Americans, with their modern weapons, were too strong. Japan was forced to open its ports to foreign trade.

The Japanese felt deeply humiliated by their defeat. They carefully noted the technological superiority of Perry's fleet. The country soon became industrialized and began building up its military strength.

In 1894, the Japanese went to war with China. After a series of military and naval victories, they occupied part of Manchuria, a large province in northern China. The Russians were also interested in Manchuria. They joined with France and Germany. The three nations put pressure on the Japanese. They were forced to withdraw. Again the Japanese were humiliated.

They took revenge a decade later, damaging part of a Russian fleet based on Manchuria's southern coast in a surprise attack. The following spring, they won an overwhelming victory over the Russians at the Battle of Tsushima.

By then, strains with the United States had become apparent. The U.S. annexation of Hawaii was one bone of contention. Anti-Japanese prejudice in California was another. A third was the obvious desire of the United States to prevent further Japanese immigration. Both countries began considering plans for war against each other.

When World War I began in 1914, the Japanese sided with Great Britain and France. (The United States joined them in 1917.) The Japanese occupied German-held islands in the Central Pacific—the Marshalls, the Marianas, and the Carolines—that stretched across an ocean area larger than the United States. These islands lay between the United States and the Philippine Islands, which the U.S. had taken over following the Spanish-American War in 1898.

When World War I ended, the victorious countries convened the Washington Naval Conference in 1921. Many people believed that the naval race between Germany and Great Britain—both sides had spent vast sums building increasingly larger battleships in the early years of the twentieth century—had been one of the causes of the conflict. They wanted to place limits on naval construction.

Despite Japanese objections, Great Britain and United States established a ratio of 5:5:3 in tonnage in several categories of warships. That meant that for every five tons of shipping Great Britain and the United States built, the Japanese could build just three. Some ships already under construction were scrapped. A few were converted to aircraft carriers, which at that time were viewed only as a way to support battleships.

While a 1930 naval treaty in London gave Japan a slight increase in allowable tonnage, the increasingly militaristic Japanese broke that treaty in 1936. They began building many new warships, including larger carriers.

The attitude in the United States was very different. Americans had been appalled by the slaughter during World War I. Many believed that they should not become involved in foreign wars. They felt that the Atlantic and Pacific Oceans provided adequate protection from attack. These people were called isolationists. They thought that the United States should isolate itself from another war. In the 1930s, they overlooked German dictator Adolf Hitler's growing appetite for territory beyond his country's borders. They also overlooked increasingly apparent Japanese aggressive intentions. After invading Manchuria in 1931, the Japanese launched an invasion of China in 1937. More and more reports of atrocities against Chinese civilians aroused the American government, which began pressing Japan to withdraw. These demands were ignored.

Japan was poor in natural resources. It had to import many necessities. The largest share of these imports—particularly vital materials such as oil and steel—came from the United States.

The United States consistently underestimated the Japanese. As historian Gordon Prange and his associates note, "To many Americans the label 'Made in Japan' was almost a guarantee of shoddiness. But Japan cared little about consumer goods; much of the national treasure and expertise went into war material. . . . In research and procurement, money was no object; what the military wanted, the military got."[1]

What the military got by the time of the Pearl Harbor attack included the Zero, the world's finest naval fighter plane; the world's best naval torpedo, the deadly Long Lance; the best-trained corps of naval aviators; and dozens of modern warships that were equal to or better than anything the United States or Great Britain possessed.

By contrast, because of the strong isolationist sentiment in the United States, there was relatively little money for the armed forces, which were woefully underequipped. Soldiers drilled with broomsticks rather than rifles. They trained with trucks bearing signs that said "Tank." Both army and navy fighter planes were no match for their Japanese counterparts. U.S. torpedoes were slow and often failed to explode. It wasn't until 1940 that the United States began spending significant amounts of money on the military. As a result, the Japanese had nearly a four-year head start.

Somewhat ironically in view of current Japanese domination of the home electronics market, electronics was one of the few areas in which the United States had superiority. The U.S. maintained this lead throughout the war.

The Japanese had much more respect for their soldiers, sailors, and airmen than Americans had. Ever since its founding, the United States had been reluctant to maintain a large permanent military force. The men who did enlist had almost none of the prestige that today we confer on the armed forces.

Americans conducted fleet exercises in relatively calm waters. The Japanese trained in bad weather, frequently at night. It was not uncommon for sailors to be washed overboard. The Japanese considered those losses a small price to pay for increased efficiency.

Most people in the United States had false impressions about the Japanese. They regarded the Japanese as having defective vision, which meant they would be inferior pilots. To many Americans, Japanese were figures of fun. They were often depicted as monkeys.

The Japanese also underestimated Americans, regarding them as greedy and ruled by the pursuit of money. They thought of Americans as too soft to stand up to the hardships of war. In particular, they believed that Americans couldn't withstand weeks inside the cramped quarters of submarines. The Japanese did not put much effort into antisubmarine warfare. They would pay dearly for this oversight as the war wore on.

The Japanese became increasingly aggressive in 1940. They occupied part of French Indo-China (modern-day Vietnam, Laos, and Cambodia). In May, President Franklin Roosevelt ordered the navy to move its primary fleet base from California to Pearl Harbor.

Four months later, Japan joined Germany—which had begun World War II a year earlier by attacking Poland—and Italy in the Tripartite Pact. The key element in the treaty was Article Three: "Germany, Italy and Japan . . . undertake to assist one another with all political, economic and military means when one of the three contracting powers is attacked by a power at present not involved in the European war or in the Chinese-Japanese conflict."[2] Because another article excluded the Soviet Union, it was clear that the "power at present not involved" referred to the United States. Even though Japanese and American diplomats were trying to defuse the conflict, the two sides were moving closer and closer to war.

Early in 1941, Japanese Admiral Isoroku Yamamoto began making top-secret plans for an attack on Pearl Harbor. His goal was to knock out the American fleet in a single blow. Much of the actual work would be done by Commander Minoru Genda, a brilliant young member of Yamamoto's staff. Genda worked closely with Commander Mitsuo Fuchida, who would lead the first of two waves of assaulting aircraft.

The Japanese started sending spies to Oahu. Posing as tourists, they had no difficulty observing the naval base from hills that offered sweeping views of the harbor. A steady stream of photographs, maps, and drawings began flowing to Tokyo.

Yamamoto faced several technical difficulties. One challenge was that when torpedoes were dropped from airplanes, they sank up to a hundred feet before rising to their prescribed depth. Because Pearl Harbor was only about 45 feet deep, torpedoes would bury themselves harmlessly in the mud. The problem was solved by attaching fins that kept them from sinking so far.

Another matter was that most bombs were designed to explode on contact. They would do relatively little damage to battleships with armored steel decks. Technicians worked with heavy shells normally fired by the massive guns of battleships. These shells were designed to penetrate thick armor before exploding. The technicians fitted them with fins so that they would fall straight down onto their targets.

In July, relations became so strained that Roosevelt ordered a complete embargo on exports to Japan. Most serious was the embargo on oil. The United States had been Japan's primary supplier. The embargo left Japan with enough oil for just eighteen months.

In September, training for the Pearl Harbor attack began in earnest. Japanese carrier planes repeatedly "bombed" a site on a small island that somewhat resembled Pearl Harbor.

Yamamoto knew the success of the attack depended on his ships getting to Oahu without being observed. Storms and extended periods of fog were common in the North Pacific. These conditions would help to hide his ships. In October he sent a passenger ship over the planned route. It arrived in Honolulu without seeing any other vessels.

Negotiations between the Japanese and United States continued. Neither side felt it could back down. If the United States began sending oil again, that would signify approval of Japanese aggression in China. If the Japanese agreed to withdraw from China, they would be humiliated.

The Japanese proceeded with their secret plans. The obvious place to seek oil and other vital raw materials was to the south, especially in modern-day Indonesia. They formulated an extremely complicated plan that called for simultaneous invasions at several sites. The key to the plan's effectivness was a successful attack on Pearl Harbor. By the end of November, Japanese troop transports and supporting warships were heading south. It didn't take long for them to be detected. American intelligence officers noticed something curious. The invasion fleets didn't contain any aircraft carriers.

In great secrecy, the carriers and their escorting ships had already begun slipping out of their home bases, one or two at a time. Maintaining strict radio silence, they assembled in the bleak northern Kurile Islands. On November 26, they departed. There was still a slim possibility that last-ditch negotiations might succeed. If that happened, the fleet would turn back.

On December 2, "Climb Mount Niitaka" crackled in the radio room aboard the carrier *Akagi*, the Japanese flagship. That was the signal for the attack to proceed.

Hardly anyone on board the Japanese ships was still asleep at 0530 on December 7 when two cruisers launched their scout planes to make last-minute observations. One of these planes was the first contact that the two privates operating the radar set on Oahu's northern shore would later report.

As the two scout planes headed toward Oahu, Fuchida and about 180 first-wave aircrews were completing their preparations. Dense clouds hovered overhead and rough seas crashed against the ships. Fuchida would later say, "Under normal circumstances no plane would be permitted to take off in this sort of weather."[3]

These circumstances were anything but normal. Aboard *Akagi*, Vice Admiral Chuichi Nagumo, commander of the strike force, hoisted the same battle flag that Admiral Heihachiro Togo had flown thirty-six years earlier at the Battle of Tsushima. Hundreds of cheering crew members lined the deck of each carrier as the planes began roaring into the air at about 0600. Despite the constant pitching and rolling of the carriers, it took the well-disciplined fliers just fifteen minutes to lift off. They quickly formed up and began heading for Oahu, now just over 200 miles away. Their primary objective was Battleship Row, where seven U.S. battleships lay moored. Even though most were more than twenty years old, they were still the pride of the fleet.

The Japanese also hoped to sink the three American carriers—*Lexington*, *Saratoga*, and *Enterprise*—based at Pearl Harbor. By chance, all three were away. *Enterprise* was scheduled to return that morning from a mission delivering warplanes to Wake Island, but rough seas and engine trouble aboard an escorting destroyer forced the ship to slow down. The crewmen grumbled that they would miss the chance to enjoy Sunday in port.

Unaware that they had been detected by radar—and equally unaware that this warning of their approach had been disregarded—the Japanese planes arrived over the still-unsuspecting Oahu at 0740. Following their well-rehearsed plans, they separated into several different groups.

It was important to precisely coordinate their attacks on their different targets. Military and naval airfields that dotted the island had to be struck at the beginning to eliminate American fighter planes from taking off. But they couldn't be struck too soon. The torpedo planes were the key element. Because they had to fly so low and so close to dozens of armed American ships, they needed the element of surprise to launch their deadly missiles.

Fuchida's exultant message at 0753 caused rejoicing aboard the anxiously awaiting Japanese fleet. "Tora! Tora! Tora!" meant that they had achieved complete surprise.

A view looking over the flight deck of the Japanese aircraft carrier *Akagi*.

Akagi **had originally been designed as a battleship. Construction had already begun when the Washington Naval Treaty was adopted. The vessel was converted to an aircraft carrier. She was commissioned in 1927 and served as the Japanese flagship during the Pearl Harbor attack. Kaga and Zuikaku** *can be seen at the very top of the photo.*

The Japanese began the Russo-Japanese War in 1904 with a surprise attack on Russian ships at Port Arthur, about 100 miles west of Korea. They heavily damaged a number of Russian vessels.

The Russians needed to reinforce their naval forces in the Pacific. They decided to send their Baltic Sea Fleet to the major Russian Pacific naval base at Vladivostok. Consisting of more than thirty vessels, the fleet departed in October 1904. A great deal of publicity covered its departure.

Many of the Russians' shortcomings were on display a few days later as they passed England. They mistook English fishing trawlers for Japanese torpedo boats. They fired hundreds of rounds, yet sank only one vessel. For the English, that was one too many. The two sides went to the brink of war before cooler heads prevailed.

The Japanese Pursuit After Tsushima

The voyage continued. The fleet covered nearly 16,000 miles in the next eight months. The crewmen were exhausted. So much seaweed had grown on the ships' hulls that they could steam at only eight knots.

The Japanese knew the Russians were coming. Their men were well rested and well trained. Their ships had clean hulls and could travel twice as fast as the Russians'. The two sides began fighting on May 27 as the Russians tried to pass through the Strait of Tsushima, which separates Japan from Korea.

Under the leadership of Admiral Heihachiro Togo, the Japanese used superior tactics and speed to win an overwhelming victory. Nearly all the Russian ships were destroyed or captured. The Japanese lost only three torpedo boats. The men who fought there were regarded as national heroes. The Japanese were especially proud because it was the first time that Asians had defeated Europeans at sea. May 27 became celebrated as Navy Day in Japan.

U.S. President Theodore Roosevelt mediated a peace treaty between Japan and Russia soon after the battle. After the negotiations had been completed, Roosevelt wrote, "I was pro-Japanese before/. . . I am far stronger pro-Japanese than ever."[4] Several decades later, his cousin, President Franklin Delano Roosevelt, would express a very different opinion of the Japanese.

A fireboat sprays water on the burning USS *West Virginia*. The ship was hit by several torpedoes and bombs.

Quick action by crew members kept the USS West Virginia from capsizing. She was commissioned in 1923. Repairs and modernization kept her out of action until late 1944. She helped defeat a Japanese fleet late that year. The following September, she was present in Tokyo Bay for the formal Japanese surrender.

"This Is No Drill!"

Below the attackers, it was a typical lazy Sunday morning for thousands of American sailors. Many were looking forward to a day at the beach. Others would stay aboard, leisurely reading the Sunday papers. A few—the unlucky ones—had shipboard tasks to perform.

Many believed that the sudden appearance of so many aircraft was an unannounced drill, designed to test their readiness. As one man aboard the battleship *West Virginia* recalled, "We saw three planes come in, about fifteen feet off the water. They dropped torpedoes. My friend tapped me on the shoulder and said, 'Now all you're going to hear is a little thud when it hits the ship.' "[1]

It made far more than a thud. A huge explosion sent tons of water over the deck of the *West Virginia*. Other torpedoes quickly followed. Immediately the *WeeVee*, as the ship was affectionately known to her crew members, began listing to port. It appeared that the vessel would turn over. A few men acted quickly. They opened valves that allowed seawater to enter the ship's starboard side. That made the ship settle to the bottom on an even keel, her main deck only a few feet above the surface of the water.

A few yards away, the battleship *Oklahoma* wasn't as fortunate. With her port side ripped open by several torpedoes, she too began to list and within a few minutes had turned almost completely over. Hundreds of men were trapped below. Some drowned as water poured into the ship. Others were crushed as heavy machinery broke loose and fell on them. Still others managed to scramble into compartments and close hatches that kept the water out. They settled down to wait for rescue.

California, at the southern end of Battleship Row, was hit several times by bombs and torpedoes. She slowly sank at her mooring but was in no danger of capsizing.

Nevada, at the opposite end, was more fortunate. She only took a single torpedo. In addition, her gunners shot down at least two torpedo planes. *Tennessee* (moored inboard of *Oklahoma*) and *Maryland* (next to *West Virginia*) were even more fortunate. Their sisters protected them from torpedo hits. For a few minutes, it seemed as if *Arizona*, moored inboard of the repair ship *Vestal*, would be equally fortunate.

At 0810, *Arizona's* luck ran out. One of the specially fitted battleship shells, dropped from a high-level bomber, penetrated the foredeck of the *Arizona*, passed through several decks, and detonated fifty tons of powder and ammunition. The harbor was rocked by a tremendous explosion. Nearly all of the approximately 1,150 crewmen aboard the ship were killed.

Among the horrified onlookers was Admiral Husband Kimmel, commander in chief of the Pacific Fleet. He had been on the phone with one of his staff officers verifying the *Ward's* action report when the attack began. Moments after the *Arizona* exploded, a spent bullet shell struck him on the chest. It didn't do anything but leave a dark spot on his immaculate white uniform. "It would have been merciful had it killed me," he said.[2] He knew his career was over.

The Japanese had other targets besides Battleship Row. The cruisers *Helena* and *Raleigh* each took a torpedo. The minelayer *Oglala*, moored next to *Helena*, turned over on her side and sank. The old battleship *Utah*, which the Americans had been using for target practice, was struck by two torpedoes and capsized. *Vestal* survived the horrendous explosion aboard *Arizona* but was hit several times and was intentionally run aground to keep from sinking.

Bombs rained down on several airfields: Hickam, Wheeler, Kaneohe (kah-nee-OH-hee), and Ford Island. The closely packed planes made ideal targets. Low-flying Zeros added to the destruction by setting additional planes afire and machine-gunning ground personnel.

The battle wasn't entirely one-sided. American sailors quickly overcame the shock of the sudden onslaught. Men shot the locks off ammunition boxes and began firing at the attackers. Many men on the airfields risked their lives to pull machine guns from burning planes, set them up on improvised stands, and shoot back.

Feats of heroism and self-sacrifice became commonplace. As *Oklahoma* swiftly capsized, four men were trapped in a compartment. What had been the floor became the ceiling. Groping in the darkness with their feet, they located an open porthole in the side of the ship. Two men slid through it as the water rose rapidly. The third man was too big to fit through the opening. Rather than trying to struggle to escape, he quickly stepped aside to let the fourth man get out. Moments later the compartment was completely flooded.

Countless others risked their lives to save men who had jumped overboard into the thick oil that coated the water around Battleship Row. In places this oil had caught fire, increasing the hazards for the rescuers.

At about 0825, the first wave had completed its deadly mission and began heading back toward the carriers. By then, the awful news had been radioed to the U.S. mainland. "AIR RAID, PEARL HARBOR—THIS IS NO DRILL,"[3] the message read. Government officials in Washington, D.C., were incredulous. Secretary of the Navy Frank Knox exclaimed, "My God! This can't be true, this must mean the Philippines."[4]

It was all too true for the men who had to face a second wave that slammed into the island about fifteen minutes later. Even though everyone was fully alert and the volume of antiaircraft fire was intense, bombs still fell on ships that had survived the first attack. One hit the powder magazine of the destroyer *Shaw*, causing another massive explosion. The battleship *Pennsylvania*, lying helpless in a dry dock, suffered some minor damage. The airfields were struck again. More than twenty bombers went after *Nevada*, which had managed to get under way and was headed for the open ocean. The Japanese wanted to sink the ship in the channel. It was very narrow. If they succeeded, it would be almost impossible for ships to get in and out for several months. After *Nevada* was hit by several bombs, the men steering the ship deliberately ran her aground so that she wouldn't block the channel.

At about 1000, the last of the attackers left Pearl Harbor and headed toward their carriers. Carnage and chaos lay behind them. About 2,400 American servicemen were dead. More than 1,000 others were wounded.

Burning oil and burning ships sent thick black smoke thousands of feet into the air. Yamamoto's plan had succeeded in sinking or damaging nineteen warships. Scores of planes were destroyed.

By contrast, the Japanese lost twenty-nine airplanes and fifty-five airmen. Lieutenants Kenneth Taylor and George Welch were among the handful of American pilots who managed to get aloft. They were credited with seven kills. Nine Japanese crewmen on five midget submarines also died. The tenth was captured.

In the early afternoon, the Western Union messenger carrying General Marshall's warning arrived at General Short's headquarters. It was one of his final stops. Short glanced at the message. He immediately sent a copy to Kimmel. The admiral read Marshall's warning that something was likely to happen about 7:30. "Just what significance the hour set may have we do not know, but be on the alert accordingly,"[5] the general had advised.

Kimmel crumpled the note and threw it into a wastebasket.

Dozens of Japanese midget submarines appear in this photo.

These tiny vessels never got to sea. They were still being worked on when the Japanese surrendered. The ones that were used during the war didn't have much success.

Admiral Isoroku Yamamoto

The future Admiral Isoroku Yamamoto was born in 1884. His father was a schoolteacher named Sadayoshi Takano. Isoroku Takano graduated from the Japanese Naval Academy in 1904. The following year he lost two fingers at the Battle of Tsushima.

Within a decade, his career had entered the fast track to higher command. In 1916, he was adopted by the powerful Yamamoto family and changed his last name. Three years later, he entered Harvard University, where he studied for two years. When he returned to Japan, he learned how to fly and became involved in the air arm of the Imperial Japanese Navy. He was assigned to

Admiral Isoroku Yamamoto

the United States in 1925 as a naval representative. His travels throughout the country gave him an appreciation of American industrial might.

In the 1930s, Yamamoto became one of the leading advocates for building up Japanese naval air power. This put him into conflict with other naval officers who believed in the supremacy of battleships. An even more serious conflict arose when he opposed Japanese plans for expansion, which he knew ran the risk of involving the United States. His unpopular views made him the target of several assassination attempts by his countrymen. Nonetheless, he was promoted to commander in chief of the combined fleet in 1939.

Despite his opposition to war with the United States, he put together the Pearl Harbor attack plan. He believed that the only way of winning a war against the United States—or ending the war on favorable terms for the Japanese—was to hit the U.S. Navy with a knockout blow at the outbreak of hostilities.

P-38 Lightning Fighter

"If I am told to fight regardless of the consequences, I shall run wild for the first six months or a year, but I have utterly no confidence for the second or third year,"[6] he said. Events were to prove him right—literally, dead right. In April 1943, when the tide of war turned against the Japanese, American code breakers learned of an inspection trip Yamamoto was planning in the Solomon Islands. Long-range P-38 Lightning fighters intercepted the two transport planes that carried Yamamoto and his staff. Both crashed in flames. A few men survived. Yamamoto did not.

27

Admiral William F. "Bull" Halsey was one of the U.S. Navy's most famous commanders.

Admiral Halsey was born in 1882. He was one of the first admirals to understand the importance of carrier aviation. He became one of the highest ranking naval officers by the end of the war. He died in 1959.

"A Date Which Will Live in Infamy"

Fuchida was the last of the attackers to depart. As soon as he landed on *Akagi*, he and Genda rushed to the bridge. They urged Nagumo to launch another strike. This one would concentrate on the oil tank farms, the repair yards, and the submarine base. The destruction of the tank farms would have been catastrophic for the Americans. Deprived of oil, the battered Pacific Fleet probably would be forced back to the West Coast. It would become even more difficult to attack the Japanese.

Nagumo refused. He had doubted that he would achieve surprise, so he believed he had already pushed his luck far enough. His mission had been to cripple the enemy fleet. He had succeeded in that mission. He feared damage to his carriers if he remained so close to Hawaii. Some might even be sunk. He gave the fateful order to withdraw.

Back in the United States, the horrible news spread swiftly. Many people weren't sure where Pearl Harbor was, but they were outraged at what they perceived as a sneak attack. Thousands of Americans swamped armed forces recruiting offices. As he sailed into Pearl Harbor aboard the *Enterprise* on Monday morning, Admiral William F. "Bull" Halsey expressed the feelings of nearly every American: "By the time we're through with 'em, the Japanese language will be spoken only in hell!"[1]

At the same time, President Franklin Roosevelt faced a grim Congress. He began with these soon-to-be immortal words: "Yesterday, December 7, 1941—a date which will live in infamy—the United States of America was suddenly and deliberately attacked,"[2] then urged a declaration of war against Japan.

Long before the attack, President Roosevelt had been openly aiding the Soviet Union (which Germany had attacked six months earlier) and Great Britain. Hitler had been enraged by Roosevelt's actions. Even though the terms of the Tripartite Pact did not require either country to come to Japan's aid, Hitler and Italian dictator Benito Mussolini took advantage of the chaos created by the Japanese onslaught to declare war on the United States on December 11.

Even before Roosevelt had begun to speak, salvage operations at Pearl Harbor were under way. As soon as it became apparent that the Japanese wouldn't return, one of the first priorities was to rescue men from the sunken ships. Shipyard workers using torches and drills cut into the hull of the *Oklahoma*. Thirty-two fortunate men scrambled out into the sunshine. Scores more were hopelessly trapped. They lived until the oxygen in closed compartments ran out. Deep inside *West Virginia*, a few men lived for more than two weeks before they, too, died.

Tennessee, *Maryland*, and *Pennsylvania*, none of which had suffered serious damage, left for the West Coast and repairs within a short time. *West Virginia*, *California*, and *Nevada* took far longer to be refloated, repaired, and returned to service. It took even longer for the battered *Oklahoma* to be brought back to the surface. The ship was too badly damaged to justify repair, especially since new and far better battleships had been launched.

Arizona was a different story. The ship was beyond salvage. Divers tried to retrieve the bodies, but it was far too dangerous. The vessel's interior was a mass of sharp, jagged steel. Authorities decided that the shattered ship would be the tomb for her crewmen.

Nearly half of the deaths at Pearl Harbor occurred aboard the USS *Arizona*. Photos of her foremast, slanted at a 45-degree angle and surrounded by billowing black smoke, became a symbol of the day's death and destruction.

Eventually the foremast was cut down. Nearly all of the stricken vessel's superstructure was removed. Some of the ship's big guns were removed and remounted near the beaches of Oahu, ready to defend the island if the Japanese tried to invade.

For several years, *Arizona* lay untouched. In 1950, a flagpole was erected on the wreckage. Eight years later, President Dwight D. Eisenhower authorized the construction of a memorial. Under the control of the National Park Service, the USS *Arizona* Memorial was completed in 1961 and dedicated the following year. The white memorial, about 200 feet long, spans the width of the ship. It is lower in the center than at either end. According to the architect, Alfred Preis, "Wherein the structure sags in the center but stands strong and vigorous at the ends, expresses initial defeat and ultimate victory."[3]

USS *Arizona* Memorial

Visitors begin their tour of the memorial in a building on shore. After viewing a short movie about the attack, they board small boats that take them to a pier next to the ship. Inside, the memorial is divided into three sections. First is an entryway. The center section has several large viewing ports. Visitors can clearly see the outline of the ship beneath them. They can also see drops of oil that still bubble to the surface from the vessel's tanks. The final area has a wall with the names of the dead men carved into the surface.

While it isn't a part of the *Arizona* Memorial, the USS *Missouri*, the battleship where the Japanese surrender ceremony was held on September 2, 1945, is moored nearby. Its close proximity allows visitors to symbolically view both the beginning and the end of the war.

USS *Missouri*

Colonel James Doolittle was one of America's greatest racing pilots during the 1930s.

Colonel Doolittle joined the Army Air Corps soon after Pearl Harbor. He led 16 U.S. B-25 bombers on a daring raid of Japan. The raid had a profound effect on the outcome of World War II.

CHAPTER 5

Months of Misfortune, a Day of Reckoning

As the grim task of cleaning up wreckage in Pearl Harbor and repairing the stricken ships got under way, bad news from other areas continued to pour in. Despite several hours of warning, American bombers on the Philippine Islands were caught on the ground and destroyed by Japanese aircraft. A few days later, Japanese troops splashed ashore on Luzon, the largest of the Philippine Islands. They quickly pushed back ill-equipped American and Filipino troops.

In the meantime, Malaya (joined with Singapore, North Borneo, and Sarawak to form Malaysia in 1963), Burma, Hong Kong, and other European colonies in southern Asia came under attack. Landings on the island of Borneo secured a steady source of oil for the Japanese. The American island of Guam—part of the territory the United States had gained after the Spanish-American War—fell on December 10. After a heroic defense, the vastly outnumbered Marine garrison at Wake Island surrendered on December 22. The Japanese were advancing everywhere.

"British and American politicians had constantly assured everyone who would listen that the Japanese were inferior people, both physically and mentally," notes author and historian Len Deighton. "Suddenly in a rapid about-face, the message changed: the Japanese were supermen, with miracle weapons, death-defying fighters."[1]

The news didn't get any better in the New Year. The carrier *Saratoga* was torpedoed by a Japanese submarine early in January. She limped into port in California for several months' worth of repairs. The supposedly

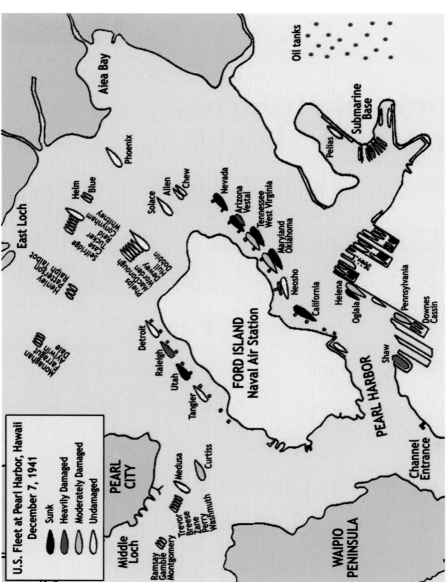

U.S. Fleet at Pearl Harbor, Hawaii
December 7, 1941

- Sunk
- Heavily Damaged
- Moderately Damaged
- Undamaged

East Loch

Aiea Bay

Oil tanks

Phoenix

Helm
Blue

Solace
Allen
Chew

Nevada
Arizona
Vestal
Tennessee
West Virginia
Maryland
Oklahoma

Selfridge
Case
Tucker
Reid
Conyngham
Whitney

Henley
Patterson
Ralph Talbot

Phelps
McDonough
Worden
Hull
Dewey
Dobbin

Pelias

Submarine
Base

Neosho

California

Helena
Oglala

Detroit

Raleigh

Utah

Tangier

FORD ISLAND
Naval Air Station

Pennsylvania

Downes
Cassin

Shaw

PEARL HARBOR

Channel
Entrance

WAIPIO
PENINSULA

Monaghan
Farragut
Aylwin
Dale

PEARL
CITY

Middle
Loch

Ramsay
Gamble
Montgomery

Trevor
Breese
Zane
Perry
Wasmuth

Medusa

Curtiss

This maps shows where dozens of American ships were located on the morning of December 7, 1941. The Japanese concentrated on attacking Battleship Row (to the right of Ford Island). They didn't touch the oil tanks or the submarine base. That decision would haunt them later in the war.

impregnable British fortress at Singapore surrendered in mid-February. Outnumbered Allied naval forces near the scene of the Japanese invasions were almost completely annihilated by the end of the month. Most of the starving American and Filipino troops on Luzon surrendered on April 9. The few who remained on the tiny island of Corregidor—the final American outpost in the Philippines—gave up a month later after being continually bombarded.

"A feeling akin to panic gripped the [United States]," comments historian Ronald Spector. "After Pearl Harbor, the feeling was that anything might happen. . . . In Hawaii a dog on an Oahu beach was even reported to be 'barking in Morse code to a Japanese sub offshore.' "[2]

One result of the panic was that Roosevelt issued Executive Order 9066 in February. Under its terms, over 110,000 Japanese-Americans who lived on the West Coast were forced to leave their homes and report to internment camps. Located in desolate regions in the interior of the country, these camps were surrounded by high barbed-wire fences and armed guards. Many people urged the president to force all the Japanese-Americans in Hawaii into the camps as well, but he did not: Doing that would have crippled the economy in Hawaii.

It was a heady time for the Japanese forces. They now had access to abundant resources in the territories they had taken over. As Deighton observes, "Japan's war plans had estimated that the initial objectives would be taken in one year, at a cost of one-third of her naval strength. Most of those objectives had been gained in four months with naval losses of four destroyers and six submarines."[3]

There were a few minor American successes. Planes from the carriers *Enterprise* and *Lexington*, now joined by the *Yorktown*, conducted several hit-and-run raids on Japanese-held islands in February and March. More important, sixteen American B-25 medium bombers took off from the new carrier *Hornet* on April 18 and bombed Japan. Dubbed the Doolittle Raid after its leader, Colonel James Doolittle, the attack didn't do much damage. However, the psychological effect on Japanese military leaders was profound. They were humiliated because the raid represented a threat to the emperor's safety. Yamamoto, the architect of the Pearl Harbor attack, quickly developed a plan that would not only destroy the remaining American aircraft carriers—sparing the emperor from any further danger—but would also secure a base from which the Japanese could attack Hawaii again. The plan focused on the tiny island of Midway, located about a thousand miles northwest of Hawaii. It would take place in early June.

The Japanese also wanted to threaten the sea lanes between the United States and Australia. They decided to capture Port Moresby, on the southern coast of New Guinea. Port Moresby would provide a base from which to launch air strikes against Australia.

On May 7, 1942, the Japanese and Americans met in the Battle of the Coral Sea. Fought entirely with naval aircraft, it was the first naval battle in which opposing ships never sighted each other. On paper, the battle appeared to be another Japanese victory. They sank the carrier *Lexington*, badly damaged the *Yorktown*, and also sank a tanker and a destroyer. Their only loss was a small aircraft carrier.

In the larger strategic picture, the United States was the victor. The Port Moresby invasion never took place. American planes heavily damaged the *Shokaku*, one of the carriers that had attacked Pearl Harbor. Another Pearl Harbor carrier, the *Zuikaku*, lost many of its pilots and planes. As a result, neither ship was available for the attack on Midway.

The Japanese, supremely confident, decided it didn't matter. They believed the other four carriers that had attacked Pearl Harbor—*Akagi*, *Kaga*, *Soryu*, *Hiryu*—would be more than enough. Rather than postpone the attack until *Shokaku* and *Zuikaku* were available, they went ahead with the original timetable. The attack would happen in less than four weeks.

It was a decision they would soon have cause to regret.

Yamamoto had devised a very complicated plan for Midway. It involved nearly 200 ships in several different battle groups. In addition, dozens of other Japanese ships would attack the Aleutian Islands in Alaska and seize two of them, Attu and Kiska.

There was only one flaw in Yamamoto's plan. Its success depended on the Americans doing exactly what he expected them to do. He believed that Midway was close enough to Hawaii that its capture would force the remnants of American fleet to attack him. Yamamoto was confident he would annihilate his outnumbered adversaries. The Japanese high command shared his confidence.

What Yamamoto couldn't have known was that American code breakers, working long hours in an underground room in Pearl Harbor, believed they knew his plan. They convinced Admiral Chester Nimitz, who had replaced Kimmel as commander in chief of the Pacific Fleet. Nimitz decided to set up an ambush for the Japanese with most of his remaining resources. It was a desperate gamble. A defeat would be even more catastrophic than the attack on Pearl Harbor had been.

Nimitz reinforced the garrison at Midway with dozens of additional planes and hundreds of men. More important, he ordered his two undamaged carriers, *Enterprise* and *Hornet*, to steam to Midway. When *Yorktown*

Chester W. Nimitz became one of the Navy's leading authorities on submarines before taking command of the U.S. Pacific Fleet. His leadership was one of the main reasons for the eventual U.S. victory. Unlike many other wartime leaders, he didn't seek personal glorification. He was more interested in getting recognition for the achievements of his men. After the war, he worked to restore harmony between the U.S. and Japan. He died in 1966.

Admiral Chester W. Nimitz, commander in chief of the Pacific Fleet.

limped back to Pearl Harbor after the Coral Sea battle, shipyard supervisors told Nimitz that they would need at least three months to repair the battered ship. Nimitz gave them less than three days. Thousands of workers swarmed over the ship in round-the-clock operations. They met Nimitz's deadline. *Yorktown* sailed for Midway soon after her sisters. The three carriers linked up northeast of the island at what Nimitz had optimistically named Point Luck. As events would soon reveal, he couldn't have picked a more appropriate name.

The Japanese appeared exactly when and where the code breakers had predicted they would. Shortly after dawn on June 4, 1942, bombers from the Japanese carriers attacked Midway Island. Their escorting Zero fighters shot down many American fighters. The fleet also beat off several attacks from aircraft based on Midway. Many of the attacking American planes were shot down. None achieved even a single hit.

Then a scout plane detected the American fleet. Admiral Nagumo, still commanding the Japanese carriers, was astonished that American ships were in the vicinity. He had believed they were at Pearl Harbor or even farther away. He began preparations for an attack. He couldn't launch it right away. First he had to replace the bombs that the planes still on board carried with torpedoes. He also had to wait for his other planes to return from their attack on Midway.

By then, the American carriers had launched their planes. The squadrons of inexperienced American pilots became separated from each other. Some never even found the Japanese.

The three squadrons of torpedo bombers did. Flying obsolete, slow-moving aircraft known as Devastators, the crews heroically attacked the Japanese carriers. They were slaughtered by Japanese fighters. Only six of forty-one planes survived. But the deaths of their crews achieved two valuable tactical advantages. One was to delay the Japanese attack against the U.S. fleet even further. The Japanese carriers were forced into high-speed evasive maneuvers that prevented them from launching planes. The other was to draw the Japanese fighters down to sea level. By an almost miraculous coincidence, dive bomber squadrons from *Enterprise* and *Yorktown* arrived high above the Japanese fleet at that precise moment—the one brief span when there were no Japanese fighters to attack them.

In five of the most decisive minutes in the history of warfare, the tide of battle in the Pacific turned against the Japanese. *Enterprise*'s planes turned *Akagi* and *Kaga* into flaming cauldrons. *Yorktown*'s bombers did the same to Soryu. *Hiryu* survived long enough to launch a strike against *Yorktown*, which seriously damaged the ship and led to her sinking a few days later. Late that afternoon, *Hiryu* suffered the same fate as her sisters. Stripped of air cover, Yamamoto ordered a withdrawal.

Nimitz's gamble had paid off. So did the urgency with which he had ordered *Yorktown* to be repaired. The victory also owed a great deal to the absence of *Shokaku* and *Zuikaku*. The Japanese might have overcome the loss of four carriers and still achieved victory at Midway if those two ships had been there. But they hadn't.

As the shattered hulks of the four Japanese carriers sank nearly three miles to the Pacific Ocean floor, they took with them Japanese hopes for a quick and short war. More than three years of hard fighting remained. Tens of thousands of men on both sides would die. Even more would be wounded. But by sunset on June 4, 1942, Pearl Harbor had been avenged.

~

The attack on Pearl Harbor marked the end of the battleship's reign as the "Queen of Battles." As events soon showed, the Japanese might have been better served by concentrating on the cruisers and destroyers. These ships, of course, were smaller than the battleships. But their speed and agility made them far more useful in providing protective screens for the carriers. As Nimitz planned his Midway strategy, he was offered several battleships, including the newly repaired Pearl Harbor survivors *Tennessee, Maryland,* and *Pennsylvania.* He refused. He knew they couldn't keep up with his carriers.

Within months after the victory at Midway, the industrial might of the United States that Yamamoto had warned about came into play. The *Essex,* the first of a "new breed" of fast, durable carriers with air groups of nearly 100 planes, was commissioned on December 31, 1942. Thirteen of her sisters also saw action by the end of the war. These *Essex*-class vessels and scores of smaller carriers were surrounded by hundreds of new warships. Thousands of vastly improved American naval warplanes became available. These aircraft were manned by pilots who were more skillful and even better trained than their opponents.

The old battleships that suffered so much at Pearl Harbor had their own revenge. In the early morning hours of October 25, 1944, *West Virginia, Maryland, Tennessee, California,* and *Pennsylvania* (along with *Mississippi*) waited patiently across the entrance to Surigao Strait in the Philippines. A force of two Japanese battleships and fifteen other vessels was trying to attack American troops landing on the nearby island of Leyte (LAY-tee). Aided by superior electronics systems, the American battleships blasted the Japanese. Coupled with torpedo attacks by destroyers and PT boats and air strikes a few hours later, six Japanese ships (including both battleships) went to the bottom. Three others were damaged. One American PT boat was sunk, while one destroyer was damaged by friendly fire. In terms of losses suffered by both sides, the battle was virtually the reverse of Pearl Harbor.

It was the last time that two fleets of battleships would fight each other. In less than a year, increasingly heavy American bombing raids—capped by the dropping of atomic bombs on the Japanese cities of Hiroshima and Nagasaki in early August 1945—and other factors finally persuaded the Japanese to surrender.

Many historians believe that the Japanese surrender became inevitable when the first bomb came thundering down on Pearl Harbor. As noted naval historian Samuel Eliot Morison points out, "Never in modern history was a war begun with so smashing a victory by one side, and never in recorded history did the initial victor pay so dearly for his calculated treachery."[4]

Most of the destruction at Pearl Harbor came against the type of targets that would play a very small role in the war. Because most Americans hadn't yet grasped the importance of carrier warfare, photographs of burning battleships struck at the heart of national pride. The images contributed to the fury that gripped the country, a fury that would endure for the rest of the war.

The failure to follow up the successful attack on the ships in Pearl Harbor would come back to haunt the Japanese. Harry Albright, who was serving in Army Intelligence at the time of the attack, maintains that Nagumo's decision not to order another strike "was the most disastrous decision ever made by a victorious commander in the history of war upon the sea."[5]

The ability to keep Pearl Harbor operational allowed American ships to be based much closer to the enemy. In addition to the survival of the extensive repair facilities and the all-important oil, the continued existence of the submarine base would eventually exact a heavy toll on the Japanese merchant marine. American subs sank hundreds of Japanese ships, many of them carrying vital oil from the conquered areas, and were a major reason for the eventual American victory.

Many commentators even believe that the attack on Pearl Harbor had not been necessary. The primary goal of the Japanese was to secure the resource-rich lands to the south. To retaliate, American warships would have had to cross many miles of Japanese-controlled ocean. Japanese airplanes, operating from bases that Japan had established on the islands they seized during World War I, and from their carriers, would have taken a heavy toll on U.S. warships.

Both sides clearly underestimated each other, and these erroneous beliefs were one of the major causes of the war. While the U.S. miscalculation would cost thousands of American lives, the country's vast industrial capacity allowed it to overcome its initial losses.

The Japanese miscalculation was fatal. As historian Dan van der Vat observes, "The manner of the attack—which Americans regarded as a treacherous, underhanded assault—aroused the country's patriotism to unimagined heights. The phrase 'Remember Pearl Harbor' became a rallying cry."[6]

In attacking Pearl Harbor, the Japanese had awakened a sleeping giant. This giant would exact a terrible vengeance.

In the immediate aftermath of the attack on Pearl Harbor, many panic-stricken people feared that the Japanese were going to follow up with an invasion of Oahu. While that wasn't part of the plan, there was actually a Japanese "invasion" of another Hawaiian island.

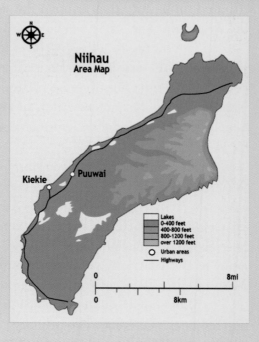

A fighter plane from the *Hiryu* was damaged during a dogfight with American planes. The pilot crash-landed on the tiny island of Niihau (NEE-ee-how), about 10 miles west of Kauai (KOO-eye). The island belonged to a wealthy planter named Aylmer Robinson, who lived on Kauai. He employed about 130 Hawaiians to work his crops. They had no telephones or radios. Their only news of the outside world came every Monday when Robinson would bring a boatload of supplies.

One of the islanders, Hawila Kaleohano, approached the downed airplane. The pilot drew a pistol and tried to hide some papers. Kaleohano took away the gun and the papers. He escorted the pilot to his house. Then he sent word to Yoshio Harada, one of two Japanese who lived on the island, to serve as a translator.

The islanders decided to wait until Robinson arrived the following morning. They were mystified when he didn't appear. A few more days went by with no word from Robinson. The islanders lit a bonfire on the top of the island's highest hill as a distress signal. By then the pilot had convinced Harada to join him. Using the pilot's pistol and a shotgun, the only other firearm on the island, the two men took control of the island. The residents fled from their homes and hid in the heavily forested hills. Kaleohano and some other men rowed away from the island on Friday night to get help.

The following morning, Ben Kanahele and his wife tried to sneak back into town to get food for their friends. They were captured. The Kanaheles demanded that the two men surrender to them. They refused. Ben, a large man, attacked the pilot, who shot him three times. Despite his wounds, Kanahele grabbed the pilot and threw him against a wall, crushing his skull. Harada turned the shotgun against himself. The rescue party from Kauai arrived soon afterward, but they were not needed. The invasion of Niihau was over.

Chronology

(all dates 1941)

January	Admiral Isoroku Yamamoto begins planning the Pearl Harbor attack
January 27	Joseph Grew, U.S. ambassador to Japan, hears reports of Yamamoto's attack plan and forwards the information to Washington, D.C.; no one takes it seriously
September	Japanese pilots begin practicing their tactics
October	Japanese passenger liner steams over the projected attack route and encounters no other ships
November 26	The Japanese fleet leaves from Kurile Islands
December 2	"Climb Mount Niitaka" message confirms that attack will proceed as scheduled
December 7	
0342*	USS *Condor* sights periscope
0530	Scout planes take off from Japanese cruisers
0600	Japanese attack planes begin taking off from carriers
0645	USS *Ward* attacks Japanese midget submarine
0654	*Ward* sends word of its attack to shore station
0700	Army radar operators detect approaching Japanese planes
0740	Japanese planes arrive over the north shore of Oahu
0753	Commander Mitsuo Fuchida, commander of first wave, radios "Tora! Tora! Tora!"—the code words indicating that Japanese have achieved complete surprise
0755	Torpedo attack on Battleship Row begins
0810	USS *Arizona* explodes
0840	Second attack wave begins
1000	Japanese attack ends
December 8	President Franklin Delano Roosevelt calls December 7 a day of "infamy" and urges a declaration of war against Japan

*0342 through 1000 are the hours of an occurrence in military time.

Timeline in History

1853	Commodore Matthew Perry sails into Tokyo Bay.
1894–95	Japan defeats China in war; annexes the island of Formosa (Taiwan).
1898	The United States annexes Hawaii.
1904	Japan begins the Russo-Japanese War.
1905	Japanese naval forces under the command of Admiral Togo annihilate a Russian fleet at the Battle of Tsushima.
1914	Japan begins occupying German-held islands in the Central Pacific.
1921–22	The Washington Naval Treaty establishes 5:5:3 tonnage ratio among Great Britain, United States, and Japan.
1930	The London Naval Treaty reaffirms the main conditions of the Washington Naval Treaty.
1931	Japan invades Manchuria.
1936	Japan renounces the Washington and London Naval Treaties.
1937	The "China Incident" (the Japanese invasion of China) begins.
1940	U.S. Pacific Fleet moves permanent base to Pearl Harbor; President Franklin Roosevelt announces extensive military buildup.
1941	
May	The U.S. Pacific Fleet becomes officially based in Pearl Harbor.
July 27	The United States places an embargo on oil to Japan.
Dec. 7	Japan launches several invasions in south Asia in conjunction with the Pearl Harbor attack.
Dec. 10	Guam surrenders.
Dec. 22	The American garrison on Wake Island surrenders.
1942	
Feb. 15	The British fortress at Singapore surrenders.
Feb. 27	Japan wins the Battle of the Java Sea, virtually eliminating all Allied naval forces in the region.
April 9	American and Filipino troops on Bataan surrender.
April 18	Colonel James Doolittle leads flight of 16 B-25 bombers in a bombing raid on Japan.
May 6	Corregidor, the last American holdout in the Philippines, surrenders.
May 7	The Battle of the Coral Sea is the first naval conflict fought without the opposing ships seeing each other.
June 4–6	Greatly outnumbered U.S. forces win the Battle of Midway.
1943	
April 18	U.S. fighter planes set an ambush for transport planes carrying Admiral Yamamoto and kill him.
1944	
Oct. 25	Five of the battleships damaged at Pearl Harbor play a major role in defeating a Japanese fleet at the Battle of Surigao Strait.
1945	
Aug. 6	A U.S. airplane drops an atomic bomb on Hiroshima, Japan.
Aug. 9	Another U.S. airplane drops an atomic bomb on Nagasaki, Japan.
Aug. 14	President Harry Truman announces that Japan has surrendered.
Sept. 2	Surrender ceremonies are conducted aboard USS *Missouri*, which is anchored in Tokyo Bay.

Chapter Notes

Chapter 1 A Morning of Missed Warnings

1. Walter Lord, *Day of Infamy* (New York: Henry Holt and Company, 2001), p. 39.

2. Akira Iriye, *Pacific Estrangement: Japanese and American Expansion, 1897–1911* (Cambridge, MA: Harvard University Press, 1972), p. 11.

3. Ibid., p. 43.

Chapter 2 The Long Road to War

1. Gordon W. Prange, with Donald M. Goldstein and Katherine M. Dillon, *Pearl Harbor: The Verdict of History* (New York: Penguin Books, 1991), p. xiv.

2. "Three-Power Pact Between Germany, Italy, and Japan, Signed at Berlin, September 27, 1940," **http://www.yale.edu/lawweb/avalon/wwii/triparti.htm**.

3. Stanley Weintraub, *Long Day's Journey into War* (New York: Lyons Press, 2001), p. 215.

4. Raymond A. Esthus, *Theodore Roosevelt and Japan* (Seattle: University of Washington Press, 1966), p. 96.

Chapter 3 "This Is No Drill!"

1. Len Deighton, *Blood, Tears and Folly: An Objective Look at World War II* (New York: HarperCollins, 1993), p. 560.

2. Stanley Weintraub, *Long Day's Journey into War* (New York: Lyons Press, 2001), p. 245.

3. Samuel Eliot Morison, *History of United States Naval Operations in World War II: The Rising Sun in the Pacific, 1931–April 1942* (Edison, NJ: Castle Books, 2001), p. 101.

4. Ibid.

5. Walter Lord, *Day of Infamy* (New York: Henry Holt and Company, 2001), p. 168.

6. John Keegan, *The Second World War* (New York: Viking Press, 1990), p. 241.

Chapter 4 "A Date Which Will Live in Infamy"

1. Samuel Eliot Morison, *History of United States Naval Operations in World War II: The Rising Sun in the Pacific, 1931–April 1942* (Edison, NJ: Castle Books, 2001), p. 212.

2. Walter Lord, *Day of Infamy* (New York: Henry Holt and Company, 2001), p. 209.

3. USS *Arizona* Memorial—National Park Service, **http://www.nps.gov/usar/**.

Chapter 5 Months of Misfortune, a Day of Reckoning

1. Len Deighton, *Blood, Tears and Folly: An Objective Look at World War II* (New York: HarperCollins, 1993), p. 592.

2. Ronald H. Spector, *Eagle Against the Sun: The American War with Japan* (New York: Vintage Books, 1985), pp. 100–101.

3. Deighton, p. 591.

4. Samuel Eliot Morison, *History of United States Naval Operations in World War II: The Rising Sun in the Pacific, 1931–April 1942* (Edison, NJ: Castle Books, 2001), p. 125.

5. Harry Albright, *Pearl Harbor: Japan's Fatal Blunder* (New York: Hippocrene Books, 1988), p. 378.

6. Dan van der Vat, *Pearl Harbor: The Day of Infamy—An Illustrated History* (New York: Basic Books, 2001), p. 154.

Glossary

annexation
(an-neck-SAY-shun)—adding a certain amount of territory to an existing state or nation.

battleship
(BAH-tull-ship)—a large, heavily armored warship that shoots projectiles weighing hundreds of pounds.

code breakers
(KOHD bray-kerz)—personnel who specialize in trying to understand messages sent in code by the enemy.

coup
(KOO)—sudden, forceful overthrow of an existing government.

cruiser
(KROO-zer)—a large warship with less armor and lighter guns than a battleship.

destroyer
(deh-STROY-er)—a small, swift warship used primarily to escort larger ships and attack submarines.

embargo
(em-BAR-go)—a prohibition of commerce and trading with another country.

impregnable
(im-PREG-nuh-bull)—incapable of being successfully attacked.

port
The left side of a ship, looking forward from the stern; a sheltered location where ships tie up to docks or lie at anchor.

PT boat
(For *patrol torpedo*); a small, highly maneuverable and very fast boat that carries torpedoes and light guns.

starboard
(STAR-burd)—the right side of a ship, looking forward from the stern.

For Further Reading

For Young Adults

De Angelis, Therese. *Pearl Harbor: Deadly Surprise Attack.* Berkeley Heights, NJ: Enslow Publishers, 2002.

Dolan, Edward F. *America in World War II: 1941.* Brookfield, CT: Millbrook Press, 1991.

Dowswell, Paul. *Pearl Harbor: December 7, 1941.* Austin, TX: Raintree Steck-Vaughn, 2003.

McNeese, Tim. *The Attack on Pearl Harbor.* Greensboro, NC: Morgan Reynolds, 2002.

Rice, Earle, Jr. *The Attack on Pearl Harbor.* San Diego: Lucent Books, 1997.

Stein, R. Conrad. *The USS* Arizona. Chicago: Children's Press, 1992.

Taylor, Theodore. *Air Raid—Pearl Harbor!* New York: Gulliver Books, 1991.

Works Consulted

Albright, Harry. *Pearl Harbor: Japan's Fatal Blunder.* New York: Hippocrene Books, 1988.

Ballard, Robert. *Graveyards of the Pacific: From Pearl Harbor to Bikini Atoll.* Washington, D.C.: National Geographic, 2001.

Deighton, Len. *Blood, Tears and Folly: An Objective Look at World War II.* New York: HarperCollins, 1993.

Esthus, Raymond A. *Theodore Roosevelt and Japan.* Seattle: University of Washington Press, 1966.

Iriye, Akira. *Pacific Estrangement: Japanese and American Expansion, 1897–1911.* Cambridge, MA: Harvard University Press, 1972.

Keegan, John. *The Second World War.* New York: Viking Press, 1990.

Lord, Walter. *Day of Infamy.* New York: Henry Holt and Company, 2001.

Morison, Samuel Eliot. *History of United States Naval Operations in World War II: The Rising Sun in the Pacific, 1931–April 1942.* Edison, NJ: Castle Books, 2001.

Prange, Gordon W., with Donald M. Goldstein and Katherine M. Dillon. *Pearl Harbor: The Verdict of History.* New York: Penguin Books, 1991.

Spector, Ronald H. *Eagle Against the Sun: The American War with Japan.* New York: Vintage Books, 1985.

Van der Vat, Dan. *Pearl Harbor: The Day of Infamy—An Illustrated History.* New York: Basic Books, 2001.

Weintraub, Stanley. *Long Day's Journey into War.* New York: Lyons Press, 2001.

On the Internet

"The Battle of Midway Roundtable" http://www.midway42.org

Department of the Navy, Naval Historical Center, "Pearl Harbor Raid, 7 December 1941" http://www.history.navy.mil/photos/events/wwii-pac/pearlhbr/pearlhbr.htm

Imperial Japanese Navy Page, "Battle of Surigao Strait" http://www.combinedfleet.com/btl_sur.htm

"Isoroku Yamamoto" http://yamamoto-isoroku.biography.ms/

National Park Service, "USS *Arizona* Memorial" http://www.nps.gov/usar/

Reader's Companion to American History— "Hawaii Annexation" http://college.hmco.com/history/readerscomp/rcah/html/ah_041000_hawaiiannexa.htm

"They Couldn't Take Niihau" http://www.huapala.org/T/They_Couldnt_Take_Niihau.html

"Three-Power Pact Between Germany, Italy, and Japan, Signed at Berlin, September 27, 1940." http://www.yale.edu/lawweb/avalon/wwii/triparti.htm

Index